"Working with Rich and figuring out our leads and how to manage our leads has been critical to what we do. In the past, when I wanted to do more business, I would go out and spend more money on advertising. It took Rich to help me realize that I don't need more leads, but that I need to do a better job of managing the leads I have. Rich's systems that we have implemented at our firm, mainly with our outbound call center has been instrumental in the growth of our practice."

Attorney James Miller
Miller and Miller Law Firm
Bankruptcy - Wisconsin

"One of the great things that Rich taught me with regard to lead conversion is that I need to have a system in place to measure the conversion of leads. Before meeting Rich I didn't realize what conversion meant. And Rich has showed me how to put systems in place to help me track my leads, down to the source that those leads came from, how to determine what those leads cost me and where I should put my marketing dollars."

Elliott H. Stone
California Consumer Law Center
Bankruptcy and Student Loan Law - California

"Rich and his team deliver results."

Attorney Tom McBride
McBride Law Firm
Alexandria, LA

"I have learned a lot. When I first started with Rich, the first month we tracked our lead conversion and how many closes we had and we found our conversion was 18 or 20%. It was really low. If you would have asked me before we were tracking that, I would have said about 80 percent of the people who walked through that door were going to sign up with me. He taught me that I really need to know what's happening in my firm. Using that information and using those numbers, I have been able to teach my staff how to better close, how to better get people through the door and ultimately that rate has increased to about 50%!"

Attorney Theron D. Morrison
Law Office of Theron D. Morrison
Bankruptcy - Utah

"The key to my success is paying detailed attention to outbound calls. This is the first time for the people to hear the voice of the law firm. And when you build the trustful relationship with the prospect, you have to be successful. Without Rich I would never be where I am right now nor would I have the success I have. Hire Rich, your life will be so much easier!"

Attorney Maria Jones,
Maria Jones Law Firm
Immigration Law - Arizona

"Richard James' program forces you to look at your business."

> Attorney Jerome Teel
> Tennessee Law Firm
> Jackson, Tennessee

"Richard is a passionate professional. The man is innovative and his people share his vision. We are honored to work with him."

> Attorney Ahmad Sulaiman
> Sulaiman Law Group
> Oak Brook, IL

"Richard and Chris are a pleasure to work with. We are relatively new clients of theirs and already notice big changes within our firm and client relations."

> Attorney Christian & Victoria Felden
> Felden & Felden, P.A.
> Jacksonville, NC

"Richard James gave me ideas which I can implement to take my practice to the next level. I feel confident of this."

> Attorney Eloise A. Guzman
> Guzman Law Firm
> Houston, TX

"Great presentation...makes me instantly want to go to my office and review current processes and implement new ones."

> Attorney Rita Kostopoulos
> Kostopoulos Law Group, PC
> Oakland, CA & Warren, MI

Discover the Acres of Diamonds in Your Law Firm

Free webinar revealing the combination within:

www.YourPracticeMastered.com

Just FOR YOU!

An INCREDIBLE FREE GIFT...

Valued at $995.00!!

Don't miss Page 81!

www.YourPracticeMastered.com

Copyright © 2013 by Automated Business Results, LLC

All rights reserved. No part of this book may be used or reproduced in any manner whatsoever without prior written consent of the author, except as provided by the United States of America copyright law.

Published by Automated Business Results, LLC, Mesa, Arizona.

Printed in the United States of America.

ISBN: 13: 978-0615836430

Additional copies are available at special quantity discounts for bulk purchases for sales promotions, premiums, fundraising, and educational use.

For more information, please contact: Automated Business Results, LLC. 1201 S. Alma School Road, Ste. 10200, Mesa, AZ 85210. (888) 375-2573

Contact the author directly at richard@YourPracticeMastered.com

---

The Publisher and Author make no representations or warranties with respect to the accuracy or completeness of the contents of this work and specifically disclaim all warranties, including without limitation warranties of fitness for a particular purpose. No warranty may be created or extended by sales or promotional materials. The advice and strategies contained herein may not be suitable for every situation. This work is sold with the understanding that the publisher is not engaged in rendering legal, account or other professional services. If professional assistance is required, the services of a competent professional person should be sought. Neither the Publisher nor the Author shall be liable for damages arising here from. The fact that an organization or website is referred to in this work as a citation and/or potential source of further information does not mean that the Author or Publisher endorses the information the organization or website may provide or recommendations it may make. Further, readers should be aware that the Internet websites listed in this work may have changed or disappeared between when this work was written and when it was read.

Contents

It's Time to Take That Solemn Vow...Again 14

Acres of Diamonds Lie Ready to Be Unearthed by Those Willing to Dig in Their Own Back Yards! 18

Don't Be Ali Hafed-*There Are Diamonds in Your Firm* 21
    Russell Conwell's Acres of Diamonds: 22
    Lessons from Ali Hafed 26
    Make a Living From 9-5 and a Fortune From 5-9 27
    The Grass is Always Greener - *Until You Have to Mow the Lawn* 29

What is an Unconverted Lead? *The Answer to That Question Contains the Secret to More Cash* 34

Can You Recognize an Unpolished Diamond in its Rough Form? 39
    A Divorce Attorney Who Gets It - *A Law Firm Without Systems Will Forever Flounder* 42

Diamonds Flow in Rivers 44
    Harvest the Data 44
    Inspect by Report 45
    Automation is the Key 45
    A Bankruptcy Attorney Who Gets It - *Every Lead is a Precious Stone* 47

Become A Lapidary - *Carve Diamonds Like an Expert* 52
   The Most Important Diamond Polishing Tool 53
   A Bankruptcy Attorney Who Gets It - *The Phone is the Key to Success* 57

Using Technology as Leverage - *Come on, Climb Out from Under That Rock* 59
   The Anatomy of an E-Mail 60
   An Immigration Attorney Who Gets It - *Texting is the New E-Mail* 62
   Sometimes the Key is Going Old School 64

Get More Value From Each Case: Increase Your Fees by Fixing the Number One Problem - *The Eight Inches Between Your Ears* 66

Bonus Chapter: Position Yourself Apart from Your Competition 72
   Become an A.C.E. 75

A Final Word from Richard James 79

Introduction

Beware, weak-kneed attorneys who consider their area of practice more of a "calling" and less of a business! This book is not for the faint of heart, the idealist, or those who view "S A L E S" as a four letter word. I hope you've requested a copy of this book because you consider yourself an entrepreneur first and an attorney second. Ideally, you know there's a leak in your bucket—one you're just not sure how to patch.

If you know even a little about me, you got this book to find out how I'm able to squeeze so much juice out of every business I touch. I'm often asked, by nearly everyone familiar with my story, how in the world I get so much cash out of a law firm and how am I able to do so very quickly?

As you have undoubtedly discovered, cash can be at a premium in a law firm. Cash to create more marketing on the Internet, TV and radio. Cash to invest in developing more referrals from allied service professionals and clients. Cash to hire more staff so you can serve your clients better. Cash to increase the amount of necessary office space, so you can provide a better working environment for your staff and more capacity to serve additional clients. Cash to finally have the life you were promised when you signed up for this duty. Enough cash to be free!

There probably isn't a day that goes by that you don't think, "I really want to add another practice area, start a new marketing campaign, put better systems in place, serve my client better or just add some staff to take the pressure off me, but I just don't have the cash to do it." Well, I'm going to show you how to find that cash sitting dormant in your business right now. And if you follow my guidelines, you won't *just* unlock the current cash available. Instead, we'll completely change the way you generate cash for all times.

I've had more than 20 years of high-heat, fire-walking-with-bare-feet entrepreneurial activity. I've bought, sold, developed, succeeded, failed, been broke and been cash rich from business. I've listened to my ECIB (East Coast Italian Bride) complain about how much I work yet how little we take home. I've sat in my office in the dark of night and the early morning hours, reviewing my financials while wondering, "What am I missing?" It all had seemed so simple to me before I got started. The fact that cash was at a premium was maddening.

I was taught in school that if you worked hard, kept your nose clean and gave good quality service, all would be well with the world. Well, someone lied to me. And guess what? They lied to you too.

Here's what I've come to believe is the single largest factor in developing a business that supports your lifestyle rather than undermines it: **Cash is king and your ability (or lack thereof) to squeeze as much of it out of your business as possible—the degree to which you achieve the highest profit point—will determine your success**. So, this book is about everything you can do to achieve the highest profit point in your business.

Just thinking about how cash affects your business is a huge leap in the right direction. There's a lot to be said for awareness. Poker players say that if you're sitting at the poker table and can't identify who the donkey is, you're it—and you'd best get up and leave before the other players take your hard-earned cash. If you want to be good at getting cash from your business, ALWAYS be aware of it. You should review your cash position every day. If it's not a positive reminder of the current state of affairs, then it's an excellent motivation to fix things.

Beyond awareness there are also practical systems, tactics, and tools that all the best law firms use to maximize cash. In this book I will share ideas that work. Either I've used them personally or my clients have used them with great success. You may not agree with all of my thoughts, but that's okay. It's part of the process.

Grandma used to say, "Sweetheart, Christ couldn't get 'em all, and neither will we." Like with a Smörgåsbord you'll be able to pick and choose what you like and what you don't like, and when you're done eating, you'll still be full.

The fact is that you can earn the respect and the income you deserve, while still enjoying a full life outside your office!

You just haven't figured out how to do it yet.

Now, before we go any further, it's important you know a few things about me.

#1. I don't offer "swamp juice in a perfume bottle."

Everything you read in this book is based on real, live application in a working law firm like yours. These systems to increase cash have led and will continue to lead attorneys to the ever elusive concept of freedom. I know because I've helped attorneys like you achieve exactly that.

#2. I want you to believe you can succeed.

It's very easy to look at these core concepts and declare, "I could NEVER do that! It's too complicated." If, after reading this book, you want to learn more or actually want help implementing the ideas we cover, you have options.

If you're interested in having my team create more cash for you in your practice based on "Discover the Acres of Diamonds in Your Law Firm" that may be an option. (I say "may" because these services are by application only. We only accept clients for whom we can get results.)

#3. I do what I teach you to do. Would you want it any other way?

If you have the slightest interest in either the home study course or the nationwide done-for-you marketing program, I'm letting you know right now that those options are available to you.

This is NOT a sales pitch! I'm simply letting you know that opportunities exist for you to implement everything in this book and that they are available to you right now.

Freedom is something that you, as an attorney, deserve. You fight for people's rights day in and day out. You have the *right* to stop working at a decent hour of the day.

I'm here to show you how.

Chapter 1

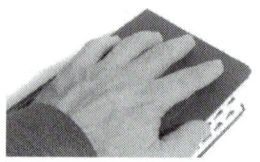

It's Time to Take That Solemn Vow...Again

Before we get started, we must perform an exercise. I need you to take a vow. You know, the kind where you put your left hand on a Bible and the right hand in the air. I'm going to assume you don't have a Bible handy, so raising your right hand will do. Please recite this statement:

My business is not different from yours.

So many attorneys I work with get this wrong. They believe that because of their location, their practice area, their client base, their staff, the color of their skin or the language they speak their practice is different from others I've worked with.

Hogwash. I've proven too many times that all law firms are the same at their core when it comes to making the phone ring and turning those phone calls into clients.

Every firm needs to attract prospects by developing a marketing plan that maximizes the return for every dollar invested. Those marketing efforts must make prospects raise their hands, whether they do so by calling, walking into your office (yes, it does still happen), sending a letter by snail mail or carrier pigeon, writing an e-mail, or talking to someone via an online chat feature.

The firm then has to convert those prospects to appointments.

From there we have to convince the prospects that it's in their best interest to actually show up to the office.

Once they arrive to the office, the firm must do its best to convince the potential clients that the firm is the solution to their current conundrum.

Once the clients hire the firm, we have to serve them so well that they are willing to tell friends, relatives and business associates who are going through similar problems that they, too, should call the firm.

Along the way the firm must charge enough to have profit available to continually serve the clients better, market the firm and provide the owner with a strong cash flow to enjoy the freedom that only a solid business can provide.

This is what I call the Perfect Client Life Cycle, and it's the foundation of all that I do.

Throughout this book, I'm going to share stories of attorneys who may be in a different practice area or a different location on the planet, but I'm asking you to remember your pledge. The lessons that can be learned from these businesses can reduce your learning curve and speed your way to success faster than a kid runs to the siren sound of an ice cream truck on a midsummer day.

The Diamonds Can Be Found In Every Stage

Chapter 2

Acres of Diamonds Lie Ready to Be Unearthed by Those Willing to Dig in Their Own Back Yards!

The Power of the Unconverted Lead

In 1987, my Uncle Bill first introduced me to Earl Nightingale's program, *Lead the Field*. It was a box of six cassette tapes that I still have and that remain dear to me.

The first time I heard Earl speak to me from those cassettes was like drinking from the fountain of knowledge. Here I was, a seventeen-year-old punk who thought he knew it all but was still full of questions I didn't know existed, and I certainly didn't know I needed to know the answers. After listening to Earl, I felt like all my questions were instantly answered. He artfully walked me through the process of taking personal responsibility and understanding that "as ye sow, so shall ye reap." He taught me about goals and the importance of working with people. His thought process on the business of success was unlike anything to which I'd ever been exposed previously. His words helped me permanently transform my future.

I'm forever grateful to Earl for being a true pioneer of the truth about success. And I'm equally grateful to my Uncle Bill for bestowing that gift on an impressionable teenager.

Earl is responsible for teaching me the single most valuable and useful piece of advice I've ever received regarding how to succeed in life and business, one I'm going to share with you. I've used this advice to achieve all great things in my own life and business, and I've used it to help my clients find the treasures previously hidden from them.

As I was listening to Earl for about the twenty-fifth time, I heard something I hadn't noticed before[1]. Earl was saying that whenever you're about to make a big decision and you're absent a role model, a map, a coach or any manual, all you need to do is look around at what

---

[1] I've come to learn this is a common occurrence when learning new material, which is why I encourage my clients to listen to audio programs over and over again.

everyone else is doing—and then do the exact opposite. His point was that the majority is most often wrong.

Think about it: 2% of the population controls 98% of the wealth. There's a reason for this. The 2% figured out something the other 98% didn't. And more often than not, the majority is wrong.

"What are they wrong about?" you might ask.

Well, that question puts you on the right track.

But a better question is: "What are the majority of other lawyers doing—or, more importantly, *not* doing—that I could do the opposite of?"

The answer to this question is where you'll find the diamonds you seek.

In the upcoming pages you'll see a survey we did of bankruptcy attorneys. What you'll notice is that the majority got it wrong.

We'll use this information to show you what you should do in order to get it right.

But before that, I want to share a story that I first learned while listening to Earl.

Chapter 3

Don't Be Ali Hafed - *There Are Diamonds in Your Firm*

If you have never heard this story, hopefully it will open your eyes as it did mine when I first heard it recounted by Earl Nightingale twenty-five years ago. If you've heard it before, it will be a good reminder of how to apply these principles in your practice.

Russell Conwell was an American Baptist minister, orator, philanthropist, lawyer, and writer, and the founder of Temple University. He famously traveled the country to raise money to fund Temple University, giving a speech over 6,000 times. The foundation of this speech, a story called "Acres of Diamonds," reveals the secret I'm attempting to convey to you in this very book.

Since Mr. Conwell's speech is now in the public domain, I thought I'd share a section of it here to make my point.

Russell Conwell's Acres of Diamonds:

When going down the Tigris and Euphrates rivers many years ago with a party of English travelers I found myself under the direction of an old Arab guide whom we hired up at Bagdad.

Said he, "I will tell you a story now which I reserve for my particular friends." When he emphasized the words "particular friends," I listened, and I have ever been glad I did. I really feel devoutly thankful, that there are 1,674 young men who have been carried through college by this lecture who are also glad that I did listen. The old guide told me there once lived not far from the River Indus an ancient Persian by the name of Ali Hafed. He said that Ali Hafed owned a very large farm, that he had orchards, grain-fields, and gardens; that he had money at interest, and was a wealthy and contented man. He was contented because he was wealthy and wealthy because he was contented.

One day there visited that Old Persian farmer one of these ancient Buddhist priests, one of the wise men of the East. He sat down by the fire and told the old farmer how this world of ours was made. He said that this world was once a mere bank of fog, and that the Almighty thrust His finger into this bank of fog, and began slowly to move His finger around, increasing the speed until at last He whirled this bank of fog into a solid ball of fire. Then it went rolling through the universe, burning its way through other banks of fog, and condensed the moisture without, until it fell in floods of rain upon its hot surface, and cooled the outward crust. Then the internal fires bursting outward through the crust threw up the mountains and hills, the valleys, the plains and prairies of this wonderful world of ours. If this internal molten mass came bursting out and cooled very quickly it became granite; less quickly copper, less quickly silver, less quickly gold, and, after gold, diamonds were made.

Said the old priest, "A diamond is a congealed drop of sunlight." Now that is literally scientifically true, that a diamond is an actual deposit of carbon from the sun. The old priest told Ali Hafed that if he had one diamond the size of his thumb he could purchase the county, and if he had a mine of diamonds he could place his children upon thrones through the influence of their great wealth.

Ali Hafed heard all about diamonds, how much they were worth, and went to his bed that night a poor man. He had not lost anything, but he was poor because he was discontented, and discontented because he feared he was poor. He said, "I want a mine of diamonds," and he lay awake all night.

Early in the morning he sought out the priest. I know by experience that a priest is very cross when awakened early in the morning, and when he shook that old priest out of his dreams, Ali Hafed said to him:

"Will you tell me where I can find diamonds?"

"Diamonds! What do you want with diamonds?"

"Why, I wish to be immensely rich."

"Well, then, go along and find them. That is all you have to do; go and find them, and then you have them."

"But I don't know where to go."

"Well, if you will find a river that runs through white sands, between high mountains, in those white sands you will always find diamonds."

"I don't believe there is any such river."

"Oh yes, there are plenty of them. All you have to do is to go and find them, and then you have them."

Said Ali Hafed, "I will go."

So he sold his farm, collected his money, left his family in charge of a neighbor, and away he went in search of diamonds. He began his search, very properly to my mind, at the Mountains of the Moon. Afterward he came around into Palestine, then wandered on into Europe, and at last when his money was all spent and he was in rags, wretchedness, and poverty, he stood on the shore of that bay at Barcelona, in Spain, when a great tidal wave came rolling in between the pillars of Hercules, and the poor, afflicted, suffering, dying man could not resist the awful temptation to cast himself into that incoming tide, and he sank beneath its foaming crest, never to rise in this life again.

When that old guide had told me that awfully sad story he stopped the camel I was riding on and went back to fix the baggage that was coming off another camel, and I had an opportunity to muse over his story while he was gone. I remember saying to myself, "Why did he reserve that story for his 'particular friends'?" There seemed to be no beginning, no
middle, no end, nothing to it. That was the first story I had ever heard told in my life, and would be the first one I ever read, in which the hero

was killed in the first chapter. I had but one chapter of that story, and the hero was dead.

When the guide came back and took up the halter of my camel, he went right ahead with the story, into the second chapter, just as though there had been no break. The man who purchased Ali Hafed's farm one day led his camel into the garden to drink, and as that camel put its nose into the shallow water of that garden brook, Ali Hafed's successor noticed a curious flash of light from the white sands of the stream. He pulled out a black stone having an eye of light reflecting all the hues of the rainbow. He took the pebble into the house and put it on the mantel which covers the central fires, and forgot all about it.

A few days later this same old priest came in to visit Ali Hafed's successor, and the moment he opened that drawing-room door he saw that flash of light on the mantel, and he rushed up to it, and shouted: "Here is a diamond! Has Ali Hafed returned?"

"Oh no, Ali Hafed has not returned, and that is not a diamond. That is nothing but a stone we found right out here in our own garden."

"But," said the priest, "I tell you I know a diamond when I see it. I know positively that is a diamond."

Then together they rushed out into that old garden and stirred up the white sands with their fingers, and lo there came up other more beautiful and valuable gems than the first. "Thus," said the guide to me, and, friends, it is historically true, "was discovered the diamond-mine of Golconda, the most magnificent diamond-mine in all the history of mankind, excelling the Kimberly itself. The Kohinoor, and the Orloff of the crown jewels of England and Russia, the largest on earth, came from that mine."

When that old Arab guide told me the second chapter of his story, he then took off his Turkish cap and swung it around in the air again to get my attention to the moral. Those Arab guides have morals to their stories, although they are not always moral. As he swung his hat, he said to me, "Had Ali Hafed remained at home and dug in his own cellar, or underneath his own wheat-fields, or in his own garden, instead of wretchedness, starvation, and death by suicide in a strange land, he would have had 'acres of diamonds.' For every acre of that old farm, yes, every shovelful, afterward revealed gems which since have decorated the crowns of monarchs."

Lessons from Ali Hafed

So what did we learn from Ali Hafed?

First, I think it's important to give credit to Ali for having two key components to success, desire and a willingness to work hard. Even though by most people's standards Ali Hafed was successful—he had land, money a family—he had a burning desire to have more. If you identified this as a shortcoming, you'd be wrong.

Money and success, and the direction they flow, are driven by a very strict set of rules. And the foundation of those rules is based in desire. You must want to achieve something badly enough to convince the Universe to bring it in your direction. This means you'll do what it takes when it's called for. The door to the Universe is opened in the same fashion as a safe. It requires a combination of desires, thoughts and actions to make the tumblers align and reveal the riches within.

A vital key to success is the willingness to do the work. However, it's vital that you work smart rather than just hard. If hard work were the only key to success, there would be a lot of rich ditch diggers in the world. I'm sure Ali worked hard to find the diamonds he searched for, as I'm sure he worked hard to build his initial success from the land that he owned free and clear. The problem was he confused activity with accomplishment. I myself work hard, but I try to first find the smart way to work and then build on that.

Ali Hafed had two of the key components, hard work and desire, but he broke other universal rules that were far more damaging to his future success. This point further illustrates just how fickle success is. I'd be willing to bet that if I asked most people, "If you had a burning desire to do something and worked hard at it, would you succeed?" the majority would say yes. Well, Ali's story demonstrates that that's not always true.

Make a Living From 9-5 and a Fortune From 5-9

Ali had the desire for riches and the willingness to work hard, but he broke a cardinal rule: Don't drop your current income-producing activity in order to chase an unproven opportunity. I believe you make a living from 9 to 5 and a fortune from 5 to 9.

Ali should have maintained his current lifestyle and farm while carving out time each day to devote to the study of diamonds—where they are typically located, and what they look and feel like in their rough unpolished form. He should have learned their value so he could understand the monetary value his efforts would produce before he went looking for them. Then, once he had built his foundation by educating himself, he could have started his search smartly, looking to generate from this new venture revenue that surpassed his current needs. Doing so would have proven his theory about his being able to make a fortune from diamonds, and then he could have left his past life behind.

By doing this, Ali would have told the Universe that he believed preserving his current value was essential to growing his net worth, and the Universe would have delivered him what he asked for. By selling his current assets and going on an unproven and unprepared journey, Ali told the Universe he didn't see the value of protecting his current net worth and the Universe gave him what he asked for—a net worth that shrank until finally all that was left was despair.

==Ask yourself what you could be doing from 5 to 9 to build yourself a foundation of education on which you could build future worth.== If you're ready to take a leap into another business, another practice area or even a new location, stop, do your homework and be sure you're not foregoing the assets you've already created.

The Grass is Always Greener - *Until You Have to Mow the Lawn*

Let's apply this to the practice of law. Many attorneys I meet with want to leave the practice of law. They believe the life preserver they bought was actually filled with lead. They don't enjoy going to their office, they ache for Fridays on Sunday, and their bank balance, family life and state of mind suffer because of it. They've come to believe it must just be the practice of law, plain and simple. They believe the grass of other entrepreneurs is greener. They believe there are better businesses to be involved in. They feel other business owners are so lucky because they don't have to face the bar association and all the ethical regulations lawyers have to deal with. I find that thought process funny.

I talk to a lot of business people, and you know what? They think the lawyers are lucky because they can charge prices that produce excellent margins, while they are stuck selling something that everyone else can sell too. And guess what? That bar association, which admittedly can make life difficult, is the same barrier of entry that keeps millions of other entrepreneurs from doing what you do. I want you to consider this paradigm shift in thinking before taking action to diversify your focus.

If you knew what I knew, if you saw what I saw, you'd understand that holding a license to practice law is like

owning a machine that prints money and never ever sleeps.

A properly built law firm can yield higher margins, employ better-educated staff, invest in very sophisticated marketing and management systems, and ultimately provide its owners a lifestyle all other entrepreneurs ache for.

Some attorneys get it. They know owning a law firm is a powerful position to be in, but they fail to squeeze as much cash as possible from their current practice area before going off to open a new location or a new practice area.

When I speak with attorneys during our free strategy sessions, they more often than not begin by telling me they are considering starting a new area of practice or opening a new location. When I ask them why, they tell me it's because they've exhausted the current business around them. If that were true, I'd support the decision. The problem is that when I ask them what their current market share is, they don't have an answer.

They *should* have that answer. It's their business, isn't it? It's not like that information isn't available to them. You can, with a fair amount of certainty, ascertain how many bankruptcies, divorces, DUIs, and lawsuits are filed each month, and you can usually see how many are filed pro se.

All you need to do is identify how many cases were filed as compared to how many you filed, and that will give you your current market share. After we do this exercise with my clients, we determine that they haven't captured even 1% of their current market share.

So, to be clear, when clients tell me they want to open a new office or add another practice area, yet they have only captured 1% of current market share, they're actually saying they think it would be easier to go out and capture another 1% of a new market (one that doesn't know them from Adam's house cat) than it would be to get some of the remaining 99% to use their services in a market where they've already developed their reputation, their referral network and a base of operations that they don't have to duplicate. It's just not a logical argument, counselor!

When we started the bankruptcy law firm we focused exclusively on bankruptcy and tax relief. The common practice for Valley of The Sun bankruptcy attorneys was to have several locations. Everyone thought that because the area was so vast, no one would drive from the far west to the far east, and vice versa.

I knew, however, that when you build any practice and open a new location, you may generate more profits, but all your pains will duplicate themselves.

If you wish to build a practice that in concert with your goals and desires, it's better to focus on maximizing the profits of one location, building systems that can be used to create leverage and understanding your numbers cold. Then, and only then, should you open a new office.

As a result, in just over two years we built a law firm that went from $0 to $3.5 million in annual gross sales from one location. The average client drove 13.4 miles to come see us—which means many people drove farther than that!

But, what was utterly more important was the fact that the owner had a business that would support his lifestyle rather than undermine it. He was now free to do as he pleased, rather than just doing what his firm demanded of him.

Unfortunately, so many of you act like Ali Hafed. You get so excited about the promise of riches beyond your current law firm that you drop your focus and go in search of a new business, or because you haven't studied the art of unearthing diamonds in your current practice area or location, you feel you must expand and end up putting additional stress on you, your staff and your cash flow.

Before going on a search for diamonds in a faraway land, it would be wise to search the property you already own. For the purposes of this discussion, your law firm is the property you own. You went to law school, took the bar exam and have been making the phone ring since the day you opened your practice. Now it's time to start sifting the sands of your rivers to find the diamonds. But, you must know how to recognize the diamonds in their rough form.

Right now you are like Ali Hafed's successor—you have those diamonds sitting on your mantel, but you just don't recognize them. Those diamonds in rough form, in your case, exist in files that you've categorized as unconverted leads!

Turn the page and I'll explain further.

Chapter 4

What is an Unconverted Lead? *The Answer to That Question Contains the Secret to More Cash*

Just to ensure I haven't lost you, let me clear up any misconceptions about what an unconverted lead is.

An unconverted lead is anyone who says:

No, I don't want to set an appointment.

No, I don't want to show up to my appointment.

No, I don't want to hire your firm.

"Why are these unconverted leads so important?" you might ask.

Well, at a recent convention for bankruptcy attorneys we did a survey. One of the questions was "What do you do with your unconverted leads, those prospects who either don't set an appointment, don't show up to the appointment or don't hire your firm?" Guess what we found?

Over 35.92% of the 120 attorneys we spoke with did absolutely nothing with those leads. Now I know that's not the majority.

However, consider also that of those who did do something, nearly 60% of them did very little, citing e-mail as their only form of communication or making only a single follow-up call to people who didn't show up to their appointments.

Very little isn't the same as nothing, but if the very little is ineffective, it's *the same* as nothing. In this case, since the very little wasn't effective, the majority was, in fact, doing nothing.

We also found that 45.22% said business was **DOWN** this year as compared to business at the same time last year.

But 38.26% said their business was **UP** from the same time last year!

21.84% had average or above average practices, filing more than 20 cases a month.

Here's what we found interesting:

All of those firms who said their business was up this year over last year or filed an above average number of cases every month did two things that the others did not.

- They communicated using *more than one* type of communication.

- One of those forms of communication was **outbound phone calls.**

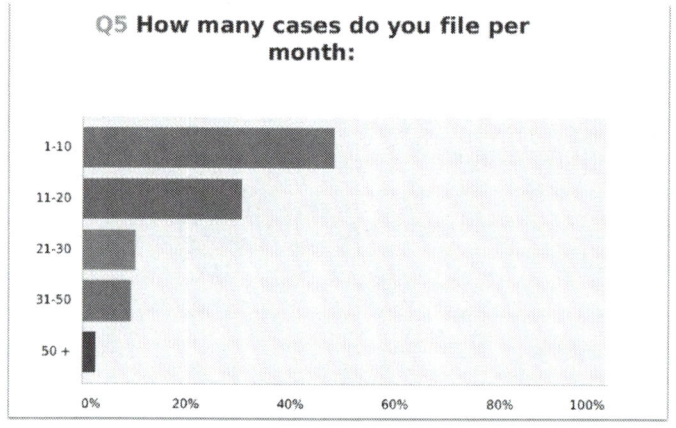

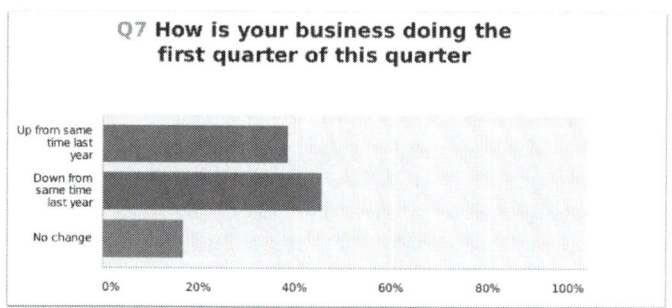

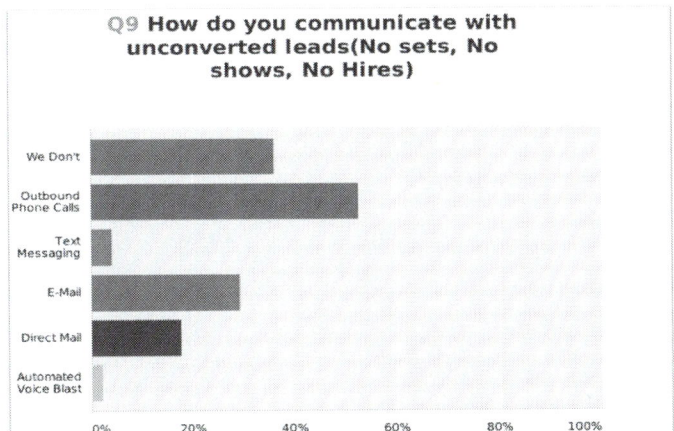

These results never change, regardless of the practice area, the number of attorneys, and the geography where the questions are asked. We always get the same answers.

We find the majority don't follow up with their clients in an effective regular manner with multiple forms of communication.

We find the majority said their business was down this year compared to last year. These are the same firms that did nothing with the unconverted leads.

We know that those whose business was up over last year used multiple forms of communication, and that they all used ongoing outbound phone call campaigns to address unconverted leads.

To put a fine point on it, winning firms use the phone and other forms of communication and losing firms don't.

Which do you want to be?

I can tell you this. If you want a firm that converts more leads to cash, converting the unconverted leads is essential.

Now, I already know some of you have forgotten about the vow you took before we started. You're saying, "Well, these are bankruptcy attorneys and I'm a divorce attorney, so my business is different." Go back and re-read the oath in the introduction. It's just not true.

Chapter 5

Can You Recognize an Unpolished Diamond in its Rough Form?

Actual diamonds in their roughest form look more like shiny rocks than diamonds. If someone doesn't know what he or she is looking for, he or she is likely to completely miss them. The same can be said for the acres of diamonds aching to be found in your law firm. As our study shows, most attorneys completely ignore what we call the unconverted lead.

I remember asking an attorney what she did about people who didn't show up to their appointments. She rolled her eyes and said, "We write them off. Who wants them? They didn't have the decency to show up, so we're not going to chase them."

Wow, we could probably cover an entire chapter on that one comment alone. Suffice it to say, I've found a single word to be the problem. P R I D E is the five-letter word that keeps attorneys from millions of dollars. When I pressed the issue and asked if she knew how many people didn't show up to their appointments, she said about half didn't show up. She's completely ignoring 50% of her marketing dollars.

Are you serious? Yep, she was as serious as a heart attack. I'm guessing there are countries where you could be caned for less, and if there aren't, there should be. When I gave her my opinion on this matter, she sort of shrugged her shoulders as if to say, "Hey, you might be right, but I don't intend to change anytime soon."

A younger version of me would have kept pressing the issue just to satisfy my desire to rid the world of stupidity. But the older, wiser version of myself understands what my uncle said all those years ago: "Rich, you simply can't push a rope." So, I just smiled, inwardly knowing that one day I'd have a client in her geographic region that would be the one benefiting from her shortcomings.

Let me illustrate this with a story. I have come to notice some attorneys take rejection from potential clients personally. I was on a strategy session with a new prospective client recently who told me, "Rich, I close most of my deals, but when they leave my office and don't hire me, man it kills me for days wondering what did wrong. Worse, I know I'll never get them back."

My first point of counsel was that he should never take it personally. When a person says no, he or she is not saying "NO." He or she is simply saying, "Not Right Now."

Secondly, I explained that in this world there are skimmers and divers. Divers are the people who act immediately when they see something they believe has value. Skimmers, on the other hand, need time. They tend to want to digest and study.

The key is not to take skimmers personally. Instead, ensure you have an excellent follow-up system to stay in touch with skimmers until they make a buying decision. He didn't have any follow-up system. "That's great news", I said. "Now we know where to start!"

A Divorce Attorney Who Gets It –

A Law Firm Without Systems Will Forever Flounder

When I first met Scott David Stewart, a divorce attorney in Phoenix, his goal was to stop being the lawyer of the firm and start being the owner of the firm. He was currently managing roughly 30 cases and he had a goal of not managing any. He had been raised by an entrepreneurial father who owned a manufacturing company in the aerospace industry, so Scott had cut his teeth in business using systems, but he wasn't sure how to transfer those lessons to his law firm.

The very first thing we did was look at the leads his firm wasn't converting. We found that although Scott thought he converted 60% of all the leads he brought into his firm, the data showed he was, in fact, wrong. It was much less. We first set a baseline from where he could judge his performance, and then we went about building a system to manage all the unconverted leads.

The end result: 18 months later Scott's business was up nearly 100% from where we'd started. He no longer had any cases to manage as an attorney and was free to run his business. And he has gotten his life back.

Is it really that easy? No, it's not easy. But it is simple.

If I were to be placed as the business and marketing director of any law firm, in any location—be it big city, its suburbs, or a small town—and a gun was put to my head with a command to make only one change in the firm that would get results immediately or else I'd die, I'd absolutely look to the Acres of Diamonds (unconverted leads) first.

In the next section I'll tell you what you need to build a system for your practice like I did for Scott's.

Chapter 6

Diamonds Flow in Rivers

In order to identify the unconverted diamonds in your practice, you'll need a system to identify and harvest them. As I discuss in my previous book, *The DNA of the Autonomous Attorney*, three critical components are required to build any successful system: the ability to harvest the data, the ability to inspect by report, and the ability to automate the process.

Harvest the Data

This can be done with pen, paper and filing cabinets, but its best done with technology. Every lead that comes in via the phone, e-mail or chat must be documented, and all the information about that lead must be entered into the system, including which lead source it came from and the outcome of that lead. If we don't have the data, we can't measure it.

I see so many attorneys get this wrong. They only gather information about people who set an appointment—or worse, they only keep data on actual clients. Since the average attorney converts less than 10% of his or her total lead flow into clients, he or she is, therefore, totally ignoring over 90% of the leads he or she paid for.

Inspect by Report

My grandfather told me to *inspect* what you *expect*. The moment you make a decision to run your practice differently, it will become essential for you to inspect your practice to assure that rules you've put into place are actually being followed. The best and most efficient way to inspect is by report.

Having a system that allows you to input information is great, but it's just as important for you to be able to get the data out of the system. There's nothing more frustrating than harvesting the data you wanted to study, only to find out that reports on that data aren't readily available. Although using pen and paper to *harvest* your data is a viable option, for instance, doing so makes *managing* that data cumbersome and time consuming.

Automation is the Key

Adding automation to a system that works is like Lance Armstrong on steroids, unstoppable. The difference between steroids and automation (besides the obvious legal and ethical issues!) is that automation doesn't come with dangerous, negative long-term side effects (like testicular cancer and constant mood swings). Automation creates consistency in your practice and allows you to leverage your time and your cash flow.

Having the ability to run reports, monitor work flow, and keep up with marketing on a regular repeatable schedule by setting it and forgetting it is a powerful position to be in.

In many of your firms, if someone calls for information but doesn't set an appointment, your staff doesn't harvest information about that lead. You just let it fade into the background.

Do you understand that you paid for that lead? Whether the lead came from the phone book, the TV, or a referral, at some point you paid to make that phone ring. In most cases, in my experience, you paid on average $50 to make that phone ring—and now you're simply going to ignore those leads?

A Bankruptcy Attorney Who Gets It

Every Lead is a Precious Stone

That's what Jamie Miller from Milwaukee was doing—ignoring leads. When I first met Jamie, he did nothing with his unconverted leads, so the very first thing we did for him was to put a system in place to clearly identify those leads and a plan of action to communicate with them.

In order to harvest the data about every lead, we instituted Infusionsoft into his practice. His staff was trained to use the system to enter every lead, every time, and no exceptions. Now we had something to work with. Whenever the phone rang, we knew the data was being collected. When someone set an appointment it was registered in the system, and if that person didn't show up to that appointment, we knew about it. If the person did show and then didn't hire the firm, we knew about that too.

Because we built Jamie's Infusionsoft application with inspection by report in mind, we were able to get immediate feedback. With the click of a button we could gain access to the cost per lead, cost per client and overall return on investment for every lead source Jamie used. Furthermore, we knew how many leads he generated, how many of those leads converted to appointments, how many of those appointments showed up to the office, and what the hire rate was for each attorney once they showed. We could also see what the average amount of money each attorney averaged as a down payment for each client that hired the firm and what the average value was of each hire. Finally, we could tell which clients who had a balance went on a payment plan and which ones didn't, whose payment failed today, how much money was brought in on any specific day, and what the aging was of each account—and we did this all with a few clicks of the mouse.

If that weren't enough, to establish a client/referral ratio, we were able to measure how many of his clients came from referrals from other clients. And we could now judge overall client satisfaction by using a Net Promoter Score survey system.

There have been books written on the subject of Net Promoter Score, but I'll provide, as a fast and poorly written substitute, a brief explanation here.

The Net Promoter Score system assumes that when you survey your clients, one question matters more than any of the others. That question is: On a scale from 1-10, 1 being the least likely and 10 being the most likely, how likely are you to recommend our firm to friends and relatives you know who could use our services?

When clients answer 1-6, they are what's known as detractors. Someone needs to call them immediately because something's wrong. If they answer 7-8, they are considered neutral. They are satisfied, but not enough to scream it from the rooftops. If they answer 9 or 10, they are considered your client evangelists and should be contacted by you via a personal thank you note and should be given a gift. These are the people from whom you should request a testimonial.

Now that we had the data and the ability to inspect Jamie's firm by report, we needed to automate the communication process. This way we could formulate a plan of action to use all five senses of communication:

- Telephone
- E-Mail
- Direct Mail
- Voice Announcement
- Text Messaging

Infusionsoft allows you to automate communication too. In the following chapters I break out how we automated the process of each form of communication. You don't want to miss what we consider the most important form of communication.

So, we customized the software for his firm, wrote all the follow up e-mails, and built all the system logic that said when something happens it should trigger a communication to either start or stop. This meant as long as his staff members were doing their jobs and letting the system know what happened during every phone call or appointment, the system would manage the rest. This was truly a set it or forget it situation. Jamie no longer had to think about what was happening. All he had to do was inspect on a regular basis that the system was working as planned and measure the results.

Within six months, Jamie noticed a big difference in his firm. When he compared the past three months of this year to the same three months of the previous year, he discovered his firm was up over 80%. He gives my counsel a lot of credit, but we both agree that much of the credit must go to Infusionsoft, as well as to his newfound clarity about the diamonds that lay waiting in his practice.

By the way, Jamie, too, had thought before this that his law firm had hit a ceiling. He believed this so much that a few years before we met he'd purchased a franchise in a completely different industry. For one thing, he wanted to diversify his investments, which is usually a good idea. But his other—and secret—reason had been that he'd no longer believed his firm could produce like a true business could. To his credit, Jamie chose the correct franchise and the new business worked. Now, Jamie has two successful businesses. And he's taking the lessons he's now learned at the law firm and applying them to the franchise he bought. He gets it: All businesses are fundamentally the same.

If you're interested in Infusionsoft and how it can help your practice, visit us at www.InfusionsoftForYourLawFirm.com

Chapter 7

Become A Lapidary

Carve Diamonds Like an Expert

Once you've identified the diamonds and you've built a system to harvest, report and automate the process, you'll want to become a master craftsman in the art of polishing the diamonds to a gleaming shine.

As you may have heard, diamonds are formed by applying years of heat and pressure to a piece of coal.

Well, when you're dealing with unconverted leads, the heat and pressure come in the form of communication.

As I previously mentioned, the forms of communication we use are the telephone, e-mail, direct mail, automated voice announcement and text messaging.

These are skills one can learn to use in hours, but they take years to master.

The library is full of information regarding each subject, and I highly recommend you dig in and do your research on all of them. The one constant for each and every point of communication is content, or what we call "copy."

Learning to be an effective copywriter will serve your business for years to come. But for the purposes of this discussion, we're going to focus on some real grass roots approaches to managing this communication.

Now, because your industry is FILLED with attorneys who completely ignore these points of communication, you can actually do these things poorly and still beat 90% of your competitors. I'm not mentioning this fact to give you an excuse to ignore learning more about each study, but rather to stop you from using the excuse that because you're not good at it you should stop altogether. On the contrary, the only way you can steer the ship is if it's moving. So get moving.

The Most Important Diamond Polishing Tool

As we discovered from the survey discussed earlier, all successful bankruptcy attorneys use one form of communication more than any other, **the good old-fashioned telephone.**

When I built the law firm in Phoenix, my very first hire wasn't a paralegal or an attorney or a receptionist. It was someone to use the phone for us. I looked for someone who wasn't afraid to get on the phone 125 times a day and talk with prospects.

On his first day, I gave that hire books to read—including the bankruptcy firm—websites to go to, videos to watch and phone calls to listen to. I explained to him what the vision of the firm was and why it was so important for him to do his job well. The person in his position alone would be responsible for talking to more people than anyone else at the firm. He was our first line of defense and in my opinion the most important position in the entire firm, with the exception of the owner.

It was his job to get on the phone and follow a few basic rules:

1. Use the two ears and one mouth God gave you to listen twice as much as you talk.

2. Understand you have two goals:

    a. Build a relationship with the person on the other end of the phone.

    b. Get the person to the next step, which is setting an appointment.

3. Never, EVER, give a price, price range or any idea of what it will or won't cost to hire the firm.

The reason we wanted him to listen was because these people, in most cases, had no one to talk to. Everyone in their world was either too busy to listen or tired of hearing this person's problems. Or, maybe this person was just embarrassed to talk to anyone and was looking for a trusted source. So your job is to give this person just that—a source he or she can trust to talk to. Ask lots of questions and then shut up.

By doing all the listening, you will make the person on the other end of the phone absolutely love you, and you will have built a relationship that cannot be beat. But, never forget your goal is to get people to the next stage, setting an appointment. Without setting the appointment, all we're doing is having excellent conversation. And while that's nice, it doesn't pay the bills.

Finally, many bankruptcy attorneys have become so convinced that people buy on price that they have trained prospects that the first question to ask when they call should be "What does it cost?" I tell the people who work our phones to look at that question as a perfect opportunity to ask more questions, but under no circumstance are they to answer that question directly. Answering that question only tells the person on the other end of the phone they are just another number and that everyone that uses our firm gets the same treatment. It also assumes you know everything you need to know about the case. But you don't; you can't. Nothing good ever comes from giving out the price over the phone, and if you follow rule number one from above, you won't have to.

And remember, this tool isn't limited to bankruptcy attorneys. Every practice area should be using the telephone to convert their unconverted leads.

If your firm isn't using the phone to convert your unconverted leads and you have no idea where or how to start, contact us today by visiting www.YourPracticeMastered.com or calling us at 1-888-375-2573

A Bankruptcy Attorney Who Gets It

The Phone is the Key to Success

When Eric Engel, a bankruptcy attorney from Washington, and I started working together, he had just begun to build his bankruptcy firm. He already had a successful divorce practice that he'd built over the past nine years, and he was ready to start another practice area.

Fortunately for both of us, he's extremely coachable. He took everything we discussed and put it into action—and the results showed. He went from driving 40 or 50 leads a month to driving over 200 leads a month. When we started he had no one calling his unconverted leads, but after we worked on a plan, he hired some part-time staff to help him.

We gave it a three-month trial. About halfway through the trial, we started comparing numbers. As I teach my clients, it's all about the cost per client and the return on investment (ROI) of each and every dollar. So, we pulled the numbers.

His firm was investing $1,200 for every new client that his staff was able to convert from all those unconverted leads.

His staff's result was a two to one return on investment. They took completely dead leads that most law firms forget about and doubled Eric's money. Not bad, not bad at all.

Chapter 8

Using Technology as Leverage

Come on, Climb Out from Under That Rock

Let's face it; technology has come a long way. It's changed so much, in fact, that it's sometimes difficult to keep up with all the advancements.

For many attorneys, using electronic communication like e-mail, automated phone blasts and text messaging sounds great, but they have no idea where to start.

The key to these types of communication is to have a system that can deliver all of them so you don't have to worry about managing multiple systems and the data they create. This is why I love Infusionsoft so much. It allows you to use all three types of electronic communication in one single application.

For those of you who might not be completely familiar with these forms of communication, let's cover the basics.

The Anatomy of an E-Mail

Unless you live under a rock, I'm assuming you know what an e-mail is and how to send one. But there are parts of e-mail communication that are important to this discussion. Entire books have been written on each part of this so I am going to just give you a 30,000 foot view on how email marketing should look.

Every e-mail has the same ingredients you must pay attention to. The first is headline. This is the first statement the prospects read when they open the e-mail. A good test for the headline is to ask, "If I were to run nothing but this headline in a classified ad, would someone respond?" If the answer is yes, you've got a winner. If the answer is no, go back to the drawing board.

The next is the copy. It's so important to have compelling copy that either inspires or agitates the prospect into taking action. I highly recommend you work with a copywriter who understands how to write a successful e-mail campaign. The e-mails should span 14-21 days.

You also need an excellent subject line. It's important for this area to make a statement that has the client interested in opening the email.

An offer isn't an offer without a call to action. Every e-mail should have a call to action to contact the office to schedule an appointment, get a free report or to waive the consultation fee. If you can put a deadline on the offer, even better. But, that's not always an easy thing to do in the practice of law.

Finally, make sure you have a unique tracking phone number on the e-mails. This way you can tell how many people the e-mails inspired to pick up the phone.

WARNING: Writing e-mails should not be treated lightly. It's best to use e-mails written by a professional copywriter.

An Immigration Attorney Who Gets It

Texting is the New E-Mail

When I first started working with Maria Jones, an immigration attorney in Phoenix, AZ, she was already doing well. She had about 10 people working in her office, her waiting room was full, and she had nearly 3,000 walk-in clients every year! Yes, you read that right, over 3,000 people just walked into her office and said some version of, "I'd like to meet with an attorney about Immigration."

Business was good. I'd say it was too good. What? How? Well, because business was so good that Maria didn't do anything with her unconverted leads. If someone didn't set an appointment, she didn't harvest his or her information. If someone didn't show up to his or her appointment or if he or she didn't hire after coming to the appointment, she had so much business that it simply didn't matter. Until one day she didn't.

The problem was that Maria didn't know what she didn't know. She had no way to harvest all this data and her current system didn't allow for automation of communication. We immediately installed Infusionsoft, trained her staff and started harvesting the data.

Now, we had the ability to decide on the form of communication best for her clients.

We decided to start with text messaging and phone calls. Because of her clients' current immigration status, many of them didn't have an e-mail, but they ALL had cell phones. So, we started sending text messages. And guess what? Her show rate went up.

Then we added more phone reps. When I met Maria she was using one part-time person to manage all her inbound and outbound phone calls. Today, Maria has a team of women who all speak Spanish and English on the phones, communicating with her prospects until they buy, die or unsubscribe. Maria has an inventory of about 160 appointments a week and it is not unusual to be booked for three weeks solid. Yeah, I know. Mind blowing, right?

Sometimes the Key is Going Old School

It's my contention that with all the new technology, some attorneys have lost focus of a tried and true system called direct mail.

Yes, I understand that using direct mail in some states is challenging, but I've found a loophole.

Most state bar associations have put advertising regulations on direct mail for solicitation. However, after prospects already raise their hand to say they're interested in your services, they are covered under the client confidentiality rule. So, if you send them a direct mail piece, you are no longer soliciting. Thus, you don't have to follow the advertising constraints.

Once I figured this out while building the bankruptcy firm, using direct mail to communicate with the unconverted lead became a main focus. I give direct mail credit for a nearly 40% increase in business in a 6-month period of time.

We already used e-mail, text messaging, and voice blasts and made outbound phone calls, but once we started sending direct mail pieces, everything else just seemed to work better. Our show rate went up, the number of appointments we set as a percent of the leads went up, and because of those two numbers the clients who retained increased. Because we tracked the results, we could directly attribute real phone calls coming from our direct mail efforts.

When we built a direct mail campaign, we used several types of direct mail:

A Shock and Awe package that we sent to clients who scheduled appointments.

Long form sales letters we had a professional copywriter write, which we sent to our unconverted leads. This helped inspire and agitate people into action.

Letters to help our collections department maintain our realization rate for money collected as compared to the value of a case.

Printed newsletters sent to all our clients. This helped us maintain our relationship and increase our referrals.

If you're not currently using direct mail, I highly recommend trying it. You'll be happy you did.

The best news is that Infusionsoft can help automate that, too.

Chapter 9

Get More Value From Each Case – Increase your fees

Increase Your Fees by Fixing the Number One Problem - *The Eight Inches Between Your Ears*

Here's a shocker for you. How do you increase cash in a business? Raise prices. Wow, earth-shattering. Wouldn't it be nice if that was it? Game over, close the book and go to work. Rich gave me all the information I need, so now I can sleep at night. Unfortunately, it's not that easy.

For some of you, raising prices is one of those concepts you just can't fathom. Right now, you're having a hard enough time as it is telling prospects what you charge. You know for a fact your competition is charging less than you and you're confident your client knows it. Many of you have a difficult time seeing yourself as more valuable than the rate you currently charge.

I get it. I've worked with countless attorneys just like you who couldn't imagine charging a single penny more than they've been charging for years.

Here's the problem: if you don't charge the right amount, you're not going be able to accomplish everything else I just taught you. The math simply won't work. So, be sure to get your pricing right.

Back to the philosophy of price.

When I met Rick, an attorney from Ohio, his average fee was less than $950 for a Chapter 7 bankruptcy. That was less than half of what we were charging in Phoenix. When I shared this fact with Rick and asked him to raise his fees, he was adamant that he couldn't charge a single penny more.

Finally, after months of trying, I had to tell Rick that based on his current cash situation, if he didn't raise his prices, he wouldn't be able to afford my services, and worse, he was headed for bankruptcy himself. Thankfully, Rick relented on one condition: if his conversion rate decreased, he was going to pull the plug on the plan. I agreed on one condition: he would do what I said to ensure the conversion rate didn't decrease.

Slowly, every month, month over month, we checked the conversion rates and I would beg Rick to raise the prices again and he would. We repeated this process over and over again until we hit what Rick feels is his current ceiling.

When Rick looked back over his shoulder, he saw that we had doubled his price to $1,850 with no difference in conversion.

Do you think that serving the same amount of clients for twice the money in your practice would make a difference in cash flow? You bet it would.

Rick's philosophy was that there was no way he could raise prices. He gave me all sorts of "evidence" as to why— from what his competition was charging, to the fact that his staff would never support this decision, to "Dayton is different from Phoenix." Now do you see why I had you take an oath before we got started?

It's important you "get" this philosophy. I'll be the first to tell you that though you can't eat philosophy, you do need your own philosophy about price.

Here's the series of questions I often ask members of my private client group when we run up against resistance to raising rates.

1. Do you believe that you are the very best at what you do?

2. Do you believe a prospect who is in need of your services would be double dumb to hire any other attorney in your area but you?

3. Do you believe that other attorneys who are charging more than you are do not provide your quality of service?

If the answers to these questions are not yes, you're in trouble. You'll never be able to sell something you don't believe in; your prospect can smell a phony a mile away. Assuming you answered YES, then by definition you should be charging premium prices for your service.

Imagine for a moment that there was a line snaked around the block waiting to get into your office. Would you have a problem setting your prices higher then?

The answer is: most likely not, because the fear of loss would be gone. Most attorneys view prices as THE factor prospects use to determine if they are going to hire you or not, but the fact is that it's just not true. I could give you facts and figures to back that statement up, but I don't need to. I just told you a story that supports my theory, and there are a dozen more stories just like it that I experience daily.

Price simply does not matter as much as you think that it does. So, get your philosophy straight, raise your prices—slowly if you must—and get to a price that makes sense for what you do.

Important Side Note

Remember when Rick said to me when he would agree to start raising prices, "on one condition—my conversion rate remains the same"?

That means he actually knew what his conversion rate was. Not, that he <u>thought</u> he knew what his conversion rate was, but he actually <u>knew</u> what his conversion rate was.

If I asked you "What is your current conversion rate or the conversion rate of your sales associates?" could you tell me? If not, we'll need to fix that problem first.

If you don't know your conversion averages, the first time someone says "No, I won't hire you because you charge too much," you'll assume everyone thinks the same way and you'll go back to the old pricing. With math on your side, you don't have to make up stories. You'll have the facts.

It doesn't take a fancy system to measure your hire rate, just plain pen and paper and dedication to the goal. Make rules and stick to them.

Every day, the receptionist should take the intake forms that people fill out when they come into the office and mark the outcome of the appointment at the bottom of the paper. At the end of the day, they can enter the outcomes into a Google database document (it's free and can be accessed by more than one person simultaneously) and send the results to you via email.

Once a week you total the results and voila, you have a running tally of the conversion rate.

Want to learn more about how this simple, little Google document can change your practice?

Schedule a free strategy session by going to www.yourpracticmastered.com

Bonus Chapter

Position Yourself Apart from Your Competition

As we look deeper at Ricks situation, I made him promise that he would do what I asked to ensure the increase in prices would be supported. To be honest, most of you could simply raise your prices 20% today and I believe you'd see no noticeable difference in the conversion rate. But, if we are going to aim at actually doubling your price, I'd suggest we do some work to set this up correctly.

There's a principle I originally learned from Dan Kennedy, a famous direct response copywriter and founder of the "No B.S. Marketing Letter, published by GKIC, which has over 20,000 members. Dan teaches about the process of creating value from the perspective of a pyramid.

Those who earn the least are at the bottom of the pyramid and those who earn the most are at the top of the pyramid.

By this principle there are more earners at the bottom than are at the top. I'd say most people generally agree with this principle. It's hard not to, as facts don't lie. But the question is how did the attorneys at the top *get* to the top?

Well, let's look at the bottom. Who resides there? These are the generalists. You know the attorneys who practice 'Threshold Law". That means they'll take any case that crosses the threshold of their office. You'll often find that in their advertising they are sure to tell you ALL the different areas of law they focus on, even if they only had one case in that practice area and that was six years earlier.

The game of the generalists is to cast a wide net. They often think of the practice of law as a commodity and many times they put a lot of emphasis on price as the reason someone should hire their firms.

The next level up the pyramid is the firm that specializes in a particular area of law. These firms keep all of their advertising focused on that one area and they don't deviate from it. They often can and will charge more than the generalist. Since they are seen as specialists because of their focus, they can get it what they are asking for.

The next level contains certified specialists. Not only do they focus on one area of law, but they have been "knighted" by their bar association as being "certified." Because of this positioning, they too can charge more than the firm that focuses on one practice area.

At the second level from the top we see the author and expert. This attorney not only focuses on one area of practice but has also written a book on the subject and has been granted expert status by someone other than himself or herself. Because authors are so coveted in our society, they have the ability to command steeper fees for their services and get them.

At the top of the pyramid are celebrities. Yes, I know, you may not be a fan of your local attorney who is on TV or radio. Maybe it's jealousy because you'd love to do it but you don't think you have the money for it, or maybe you chalk up this media success to good looks, etc., or maybe you think that they shouldn't turn the practice of law into a side show. Or maybe you'd love to do it but are just afraid of risking what you consider a large bet on an unsure thing. Whatever the case, I can tell you that celebrities make more because they can charge more.

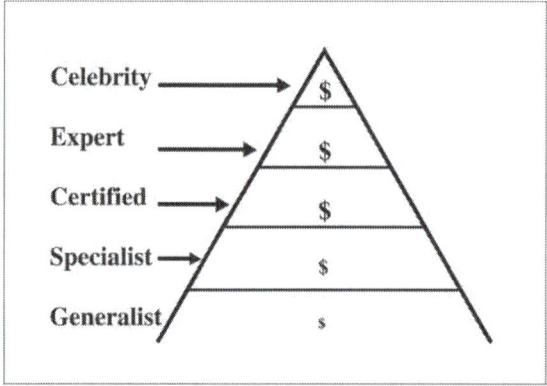

The good news is that there is a very clear path to success when you're looking to charge more in your practice.

Become an A.C.E.

I call this principle A.C.E.—Authorship, Celebrity and Expert. How do you get to there? By writing a book.

Yes, I want you to write a book. Not an e-book but an actual physical book much like this one you're reading right now. Trust me; it's not as big of a deal as you think it is. But, *everyone* thinks it's a big deal, which is exactly the point.

The average Joe believes that writing a book is akin to climbing Mount Everest or running a marathon— and that's a good thing. When you write a book, they think you've done something superhuman. This gives you a status point that separates you from your competition. In Phoenix, they've given away over 15,000 of these books and people love them. They come into the office with the book underlined, highlighted and with questions written in the margins. They assume they have the answers because, well, they wrote the book!

Let me tell you a story of my own that will further illustrate the power of a book.

After I wrote my first book, *The DNA of the Autonomous Attorney*, I was sure to have a copy with me at all times. When someone asked me for my business card, I'd hand that person a book. Well, on one occasion I was invited to one of the largest law firms in Phoenix. Now I normally don't work with large law firms because they are filled with committees and red tape that prevent them from making decisions very quickly. But, on this occasion I was referred to this firm by the owner's son, so I went.

Upon greeting the founding partner, I handed him a copy of my book as a business card. He quickly thumbed through the book and then he and I proceeded to have a wonderful conversation. He told me the story of how his firm was created, his philosophy of how a law firm should be run and his dreams for the future. We had lunch together and before leaving that day he told me that he wanted to tell me something. He said, "Rich, in all my years, not a single vendor or consultant ever handed me a book as their business card like you did today. And you know what? I'm going to read that book, and in many ways I feel I owe you according to the laws of reciprocity. So I'll tell you what, I'm going to give you a meeting with my marketing director and maybe we'll find a way to do business together."

Now, if it had ended there, it would be a success story. But, the very next morning I got an email from this attorney stating my book had inspired him so much that he'd started to write his very own. As a matter of a fact, he had attached a copy of the first chapter and wondered if I'd be kind enough to give him my opinion of it!

Look, I'm long past wondering if this works. I *know* it works. So, sit down and start writing your book today. If you don't know where to start, visit my site, www.YourPracticeMastered.com.

That covers the A – Authorship. I'm going to go out of order and talk about "E" for expert next because it will make it easier for you to see how to use the letter "C."

How does one become an expert? Well, the mere fact that you're an attorney makes you an expert. Some of you took the next step and got a Legal Master's degree or qualified as a certified specialist with your bar association.

These are good starts, but nothing trumps the one ability you cannot receive on your own, credibility. It's the one ability that must be granted to you by someone else. Someone else that people know like and trust saying you're an expert is better than you saying you're an expert. When you combine the expert endorsement from a trusted source with the first principle of authorship, you achieve true expert status.

Why? Because being an author gives you authority. The word "author" is literally the root of the word "authority." So, what do you do with all this value? You have someone interview you and you record it, with video, audio or preferably both.

Now that we know how to create expert status, what do we do with it? Well, let's focus on Celebrity. We all inherently know that celebrities earn more than the rest of us. Why? As motivational speaker Jim Rhone would say, "Don't sign up for that class."

I really don't care why they get paid more. What I care about is how use that in my business. How can I create celebrity? I could borrow celebrity by using dead celebrities. It's done all the time. Just look at Elvis in Vegas or more apropos, Johnnie Cochran in the practice of law. But I'd prefer to make my client the celebrity.

So, how do we do that? The first question we have to ask ourselves is "Where are celebrities found?" The answer is the stage and the screen. The bigger the stage or the bigger the screen, the bigger the celebrity. So how do we get on the stage or the screen? The answer lies in the first letter of the acronym, "Authorship." If you want to get a speaking gig, be sure to lead in with your book. If you want to get on TV or radio, use your book as an entry point to get interviewed.

It's no secret that celebrity status helps with business and because of this so many people are looking for free ways to get on TV and radio. The producers of these shows are inundated with public relations press releases and have a difficult time wading through the crap to find the true gems. These press releases have become uninvited pests. I'm suggesting you position yourself as a welcomed guest. And the way to do that is with a copy of your book. Try it, and you'll be surprised at what happens.

A Final Word from Richard James

I am honored that you obtained a copy of my latest book. I want you to know that I don't take lightly my responsibility to provide insight.

Before I accept advice from someone, I want to know what his or her personal standards are. In the event you feel the same way, I thought I should let you know where I stand.

I truly believe attorneys can create a practice that will support their lifestyle rather than undermine it.

I believe that there is a right way to do things—and that those things *must* be done right to maximize results. I guarantee that I will show you the systems that work and that will achieve actual results for you and your business.

I believe in being on time, every time. If I miss a call or a deadline, you can bet that I'm either in the hospital or dead. I never lie, cheat, or steal; always use please and thank you; and abide by the Golden Rule of "Treat others as you wish to be treated."

If I agree to get something done, you can rest assured that it's going to happen. When I do screw up—and yes, it does happen—I admit my mistake, clean it up, and move on.

If, after reading this book, you are looking to work with a person who believes in doing things right, having full accountability, and backing it up with action that actually gets results, give me a call.

888-375-2573

Building a better business, one system at a time...

Incredible FREE special offer...

Step #1: Simply go to: www.YourPracticeMastered.com

Step #2: Register for the webinar

Step #3: Watch the entire webinar

Step #4: Select a timeslot for your *FREE, 60-MINUTE, ONE FULL HOUR* Strategy Session to discuss <u>YOUR PRACTICE</u>!

If you don't find value in this 60-minute call, we'll *PAY YOU $100 FOR YOUR TIME!!!*

Valued at $995.00!!!

Made in the USA
Charleston, SC
22 June 2014